Just Joking CATS

NATIONAL
GEOGRAPHIC
KiDS

Just Joking CATS

Kelley Miller

NATIONAL GEOGRAPHIC
WASHINGTON, D.C.

The soft part of a cat's nose has a unique pattern, just like a human fingerprint.

KNOCK,

KNOCK.

Who's there?
Butter.
Butter who?
Butter let me in.
I have jokes
to share!

Famous ★★
★ Feline

6

NAME: Grumpy Cat
BREED: Unknown
(but her coat is similar to a snowshoe cat)

SUPERSTAR STATUS:

Don't tell Grumpy Cat to cheer up. Her world-famous frown and cranky messages have earned her a fortune and millions of fans. Although her mother was a standard domestic shorthair, Grumpy Cat's permanent pout and short stature were likely caused by a genetic mutation called dwarfism. Grumpy Cat would probably hate to admit it, but there are actually two things that make her very happy: being held and being petted by her owner.

Grumpy Cat has a brother named Pokey. He looks only slightly more cheerful than his sister.

Grumpy Cat's real name is Tardar Sauce.

Grumpy Cat loves to hide behind curtains. Maybe she's practicing for her big entrance on a future awards show—Congratulations to the winner of Grump of the Year!

Q

How did the cat feel about the scary movie?

A

It was completely hair-raising.

TONGUE TWISTER!

Say this fast three times:

Not a lot of ocelots.

Q

What is a cat's favorite party snack?

Mouse Krispies Treats.

A

Q

Why did the **cat** get sent to the **principal's office?**

She was a cheetah.

A

8

KNOCK, KNOCK.

Who's there?
Annie
Annie who?
Annie body want to play hide-and-sleep?

A cat spends two-thirds of each day sleeping.

Q Why did the leopard spit out the clown?

A He tasted funny.

Q How does a **lion** greet a **gazelle**?

A "Pleased to eat you!"

Naughty PETS

CAUGHT ON CAMERA

FEEL THE POWER OF MY SPINNING HEADLOCK ELBOW DROP!

NAME Zumba

FAVORITE ACTIVITY
Perfecting wrestling moves with his pal Doggie Dynamo

FAVORITE TOY
Dwayne "The Rock" Johnson action figure

PET PEEVE Tail pulling

11

JOSHUA: Did your cat like the new movie?
LAURA: Yes, he gave it two paws up!

Say this fast three times:

Wow, cats chow down now.

Cat TALK

THERE'S A HAIR IN THIS SANDWICH. MAKE ME ANOTHER ONE.

Q Who do cats **send** their wish lists to at **Christmas?**

A Santa Claws.

About 20 muscles in each ear let cats rotate both ears in different directions at the same time. This enables them to pinpoint the source of a sound.

KNOCK, KNOCK.

Who's there?
Ear.
Ear who?
Ear I am!
Ready to go!

13

14

Cat
TALK

AMELIA: Why are cats better pets than toads?
BEN: I don't know, why?
AMELIA: Cats have nine lives, and toads croak every night.

Q Why are **kittens** so good at playing the **drums?**

A They're naturals at *purr*-cussion instruments!

Q

What do you get when you cross a **snow leopard** and a **snowman?**

A Frostbite.

Q What is a cat's favorite flower?

A A tiger lily.

Say this fast three times:

Cool cats cook cute cat cookies.

Q What color does a cat like best?

A Purr-ple.

I SAW A LINE FORMING, SO I GOT IN IT. WE'RE WAITING ON CAT TREATS, RIGHT? BECAUSE THE OTHERS AGREED I COULD HAVE ALL OF THEM. THANKS.

Cat TALK

KNOCK, KNOCK.

Who's there?
Ocelot.
Ocelot who?
Ocelot of lights on inside, so I know you're home.

Ocelots clean all the feathers and fur off their food before they eat it.

Most cats catch more mice than birds. That's partly because birds can spot a cat's tail twitching from up above.

KNOCK, KNOCK.

Who's there?
Irish.
Irish who?
Irish you'd let me outside more often to chase the birds.

20

What happens when you cross a lion with a watchdog? **Q**

The postman stops delivering your mail. **A**

OH YEAH? I ONCE CAUGHT A MOUSE THIS BIG!

Cat TALK

Cats are the world's most popular pets, with more than 400 million in the world.

23

Say this fast three times:

She sells serval shirts.

Q What did the tiger yell when it jumped into the swimming pool?

A "Furball!"

Q

Where do tigers exercise?

A Jungle gyms.

Q What did the mama cat pack for her kitten's lunch?

A A *meow*-naise sandwich.

NAME: Cooper

BREED: American shorthair

SUPERSTAR STATUS:

Cooper's surprising artistic talent has led to photo exhibits across the United States and a world of human fans. Quite a feat when you're only six inches (15 cm) off the ground. Once a week, Cooper wears a custom-made digital camera that automatically snaps a picture every two minutes. He crawls under bushes, leaps onto fences, and captures images of the neighborhood dogs. Cooper's authentic street-style photography has captured abstract views of nature, a fellow (human) photographer, and even another cat that was having a really bad hair day. It's all just another day in the neighborhood for this tomcat.

His favorite treats are freeze-dried shrimp.

Cooper also shoots videos.

Fans can purchase prints of Cooper's work, which he signs with his *paw*-tograph.

26

Famous ★★
★ Feline

27

Why is the snow leopard so popular?

Snow leopards live at elevations as high as 18,000 feet (5,500 m). That's almost as high as North America's tallest peak: Denali (formerly Mount McKinley), in Alaska, U.S.A.

A Because it's the coolest cat around.

KNOCK, KNOCK.

Who's there?
The Vet.
Uh, nobody's home.
Go away!

A cat's heart beats twice as fast as a human's.

Q What do you call a cat that has been caught by the police?

A A purr-petrator.

WELL, IF HE SAYS I NEED BRACES ...

Cat TALK

31

AM I A KITTEN OR A FROG? YOU HAVE CAT TO BE KITTEN ME.

Cat TALK

Q How do you make a **cheetah disappear?**

A Use spot remover.

TONGUE TWISTER!

Say this fast three times:

A kitty cat bought bright bric-a-bracs.

Q What sport do tigers play?

A Fast-pitch furball.

Q What did the cheetah say after winning the race?

A "I'm feline great!"

KNOCK, KNOCK.

Who's there?
Tamara.
Tamara who?
Tamara I want tuna for dinner!

A study showed that cats eat about 15 percent less food in summer than in winter.

35

Q

What singer did the cat listen to on the radio?

A

Kitty Purry.

Cat
TALK

MOM, WHY DON'T THE PHOTOGRAPHERS TAKE PHOTOS OF ME? LOOK AT THIS AWARD-WINNING SMILE!

KNOCK, KNOCK.

Who's there?
Needle.
Needle who?
Needle little kitten
for snuggling?

Some dogs are
allergic to cats!

38

Naughty PETS

CAUGHT ON CAMERA

NAME Elton

FAVORITE ACTIVITY
Composing piano *meow*-sic

FAVORITE TOY
Piano pedals

PET PEEVE Keyboard cover

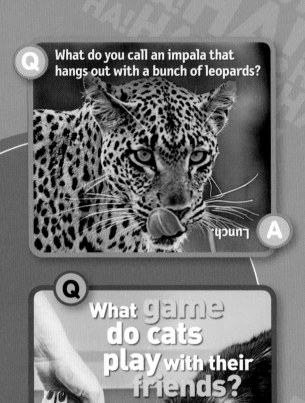

Q What do you call an impala that hangs out with a bunch of leopards?

A Lunch.

Q What game do cats play with their friends?

A Follow the Laser.

All cats have tongues covered with tiny spikes to help them comb their fur, or in the case of big cats, to tear meat off of bones.

KNOCK, KNOCK.

Who's there?
Harmony.
Harmony who?
Harmony knock-knock jokes are you willing to hear?

41

A Cat's To-Do List:

1. Eat
2. Nap
3. Sharpen claws on chair
4. Repeat steps 1 through 3
5. Sit on owner's head

Q Why do **cats drink coffee?**

A It makes them *purr-ky.*

A boy in a movie theater sits down next to a cat. The boy asks, "How did you get in here?" The cat says, "I walked." The boy, unsatisfied by that answer, asks, "But what are you doing at the movies?" The cat replies, "I read the book and heard the movie was pretty good, too!"

A cat's whiskers are the same width as its body to help it determine if it can fit through a tight opening.

Q

How does a cat type in its name online?

A By typing: A Tab B.

Say this fast three times:

Lion's yarn, lynx's arm.

Q

What do you call a cat with a wooden leg?

A Peggy.

Q

What has **black**, **white**, and **orange** stripes?

A An orange tabby riding a zebra.

46

Fishing cats have webbed paws that help them swim and hunt in the water.

ROB: Have you seen a catfish?
BETHANY: No, but it must be hard to hold the rod in its paws!

YOU SAID THERE'D BE TACOS. I'M WAITING.

Cat TALK

Q

Why did the scaredy-cat cross the road?

A

It was too chicken not to.

A cat takes its dog to the park. Another dog owner asks, "Is that your dog?" The cat says, "Of course. I'm not going to fetch my own paper."

Cats are intelligent. They can be taught to jump through hoops, walk on a high wire, and even "strum" a guitar.

Famous ★★ ★Feline

NAME: Waffles

BREED: Scottish fold

SUPERSTAR STATUS:

Waffles's owners couldn't have a dog, so they picked something even better—a cat that resembles one. Scottish folds, named for their folded ears, have a habit of striking odd poses. It's no surprise then that Waffles's millions of followers enjoy seeing him curled up into the cutest trapezoid on the Internet. The real upside to so many fans? More people to give him tummy rubs!

He's a picky eater and prefers chicken-flavored cat treats over actual waffles.

His motto is "Dogs need to know many tricks, cute cats need only one."

Waffles is also a movie critic. And what movie achieved the coveted five paws up? *Fur-ozen.*

Although the bobcat is rarely seen, it is the most common wildcat in North America.

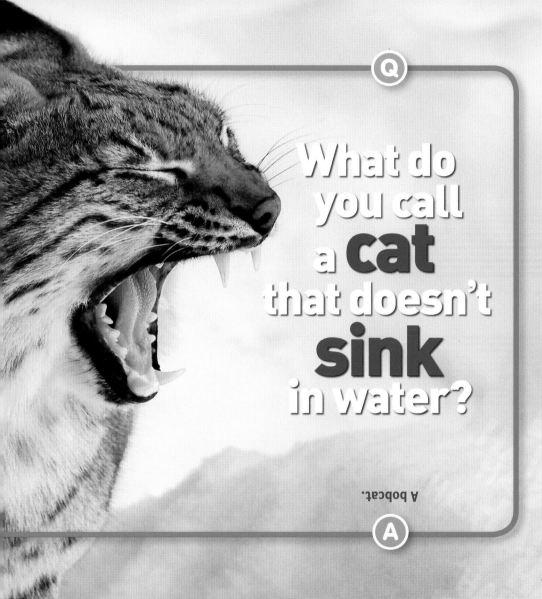

What do you call a cat that doesn't sink in water?

A bobcat.

Q What do alley cats do on the weekends?

A They go bowling.

TONGUE TWISTER!

Say this fast three times:

Louder clowder.

Q What kind of jewelry do fancy cats wear?

A Purr-l necklaces.

Q What do you call a cat in a turtleneck?

A Stuck.

The word for "cat" is *mio* in Chinese, *gatto* in Italian, *poes* in Dutch, and *kedi* in Turkish.

KNOCK, KNOCK.

Who's there?
Al.
Al who?
Al be hiding in your shoe!

55

IS THERE SOMETHING IN MY TEETH?
WHOA, YEAH. HAVE YOU BEEN TO THE DENTIST, LIKE, EVER? YOUR TEETH ARE FUNKY!
Cat TALK

Q Why is it hard to watch a movie at home with a cat?

A It's always hitting the *paws* button.

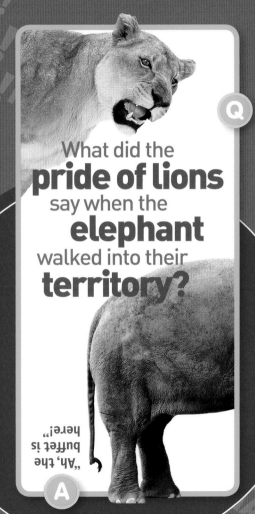

Q What did the **pride of lions** say when the **elephant** walked into their **territory?**

A "Ah, the buffet is here!"

Lions are the only cats
that live in groups.

59

Q

Why did the **kitten** nibble on the **lampshade?**

A

It wanted a light snack.

KATE: My cat is reading a new book.
JAMES: Really? What's the title?
KATE: *Hairy Potter and the Goblet of Cat Food.*

KNOCK, KNOCK.

Who's there?
Kent.
Kent who?
Kent you tell from my meow?

Cats do not like prolonged eye contact, so don't stare into their eyes. They might think you are threatening them.

Q Why do cats claw a couch and not a chair?

A Because the chair is armed.

TONGUE TWISTER!

Say this fast three times:

Cara's caracal.

Q What is the motto of a cat with a great attitude?

A "I got a new *purr*coat and I'm feline fine!"

Q What do **cats** in **France** eat for **dessert?**

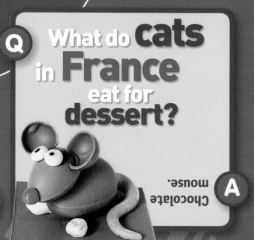

A Chocolate mouse.

62

KNOCK, KNOCK.

Who's there?
Violet.
Violet who?
Violet any more time pass? Open the door so we can hug!

Persian cats have such flat faces that they can't move their whiskers at all.

Q Why did the **cougar** eat the **gymnast?**

A The vet put it on a well-balanced diet.

ANNA: What's the difference between a lion and a lecture?
MARCUS: I don't know. What?
ANNA: One roars and the other bores.

NauGHty PETS

CAUGHT ON CAMERA

SEE? THIS POT IS WAY TOO BIG FOR THESE FLOWERS.

NAME Petunia

FAVORITE ACTIVITY
Repotting plants

FAVORITE TOY
Big hill of soil to dig in

PET PEEVE Sprinklers

Human food technologists actually taste cat and dog chow for pet food companies.

Q How did the **police** catch the **cat burglar?**

A With catnip.

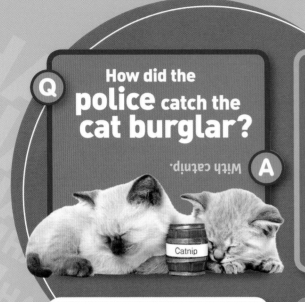

Catnip

Say this fast three times:

Four furry felines phoned Frances.

Q What is smarter than a talking cat?

A Nothing. At least that's what my cat told me.

Q Who likes extreme sports more, a rooster or an ocelot?

A The ocelot, because it's no chicken.

WOW, YOU ARE REALLY BAD AT HIDE-AND-SEEK.

Cat TALK

Lynx kittens become independent by the time they're a year old.

NAME: Princess Monster Truck

BREED: Unknown

(but she has some features similar to a Persian cat)

SUPERSTAR STATUS:

The only kind of monster you'd want to find in a dark alley is the Princess Monster Truck kind. Fortunately, her owners weren't scared off when they rescued the black cat with the uniquely cute underbite. Her Instagram followers enjoy seeing her snuggle piles of socks and sit in boxes of shirts. She certainly gives them her Princess Monster Truck touch— of cat hair. As her popularity has grown, so has Princess Monster Truck's ability to help other cool cats find their permanent homes. Now that's definitely worth thousands of likes.

She hates baths, but doesn't mind having her teeth brushed.

Her nicknames are "Monster" and "The Monst."

Princess Monster Truck loves the guitar. She'll sit next to someone playing and purr.

72

Famous ★★
★ Feline

Q What did the cheetah name its music group?

A Spot and the Polka Dots.

WILL: What do cats do when a light breaks?
KYLE: They call someone to fix it?
WILL: No, they just use their night vision.

At about seven weeks old, kittens learn the signs for inviting each other to play.

KNOCK, KNOCK.

Who's there?
Wanda.
Wanda who?
Wanda around the house with me?

Q If a **human** with two legs is a **biped,** what's a **tiger** with four legs?

A Stri-ped!

A tiger's skin is striped, like its fur.

Q

If firemen have Dalmatians, who do cats work with?

A Claw enforcement officers.

Say this fast three times:

Flora feeds Fluffy fresh fish.

Q Did you hear about the cheetah whose spots turned into stripes?

A It was a purr-plexing case.

Q

Which bird did the neighborhood cat eat?

A It was a swallow.

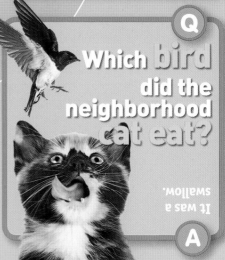

Cats hunt what they can get: rats in New York City, lizards in Georgia, and baby turtles on Africa's Seychelles islands.

79

Q

How did the cat shrink?

A

It drank condensed milk.

Q What is the worst kind of cat to encounter?

A A catastrophe.

On a Cat's Reading List:

- *9 Lives, 900 Naps* by I. B. Sleepen
- *A Tail of Two Kitties* by Clawdette Abby
- *From Class Clown to King of the Jungle* by Dee Leon
- *How to Speak Human* by Sue Pereezy
- *Fido: Friend or Foe?* by Ima Pettu
- *A Field of Furball Dreams* by Harry Katz

Q

What did the
lion say when
the baboon
jumped on
its back?

"Lunch is on
me today!"

A

A policeman pulls over a driver
with a leopard in his front
seat. The officer says, "Sir,
you need to take that animal
to the zoo." The driver says,
"I'm on my way!" Two hours
later, the officer pulls over the
driver and leopard again. The
officer says, "Sir, didn't I tell
you to take that leopard to
the zoo?" The driver replies
"I did. He had a great time.
Now he wants to go
to a steak house
for dinner."

84

A group of adult cats is called a clowder.

Q What do you call a cat that's in a bad mood?

A Huffy.

Q What do you call a cross between a cat and a balloon?

A Puffy.

Q What do you call a cat that has a cold?

A Stuffy.

Q What do you call a cat that's caught in a windstorm?

A Fluffy.

Q What do you call a cat that lifts a lot of weights?

A Buffy.

1.5KG   1.5KG

Q What did the cat say after hearing too many bad jokes?

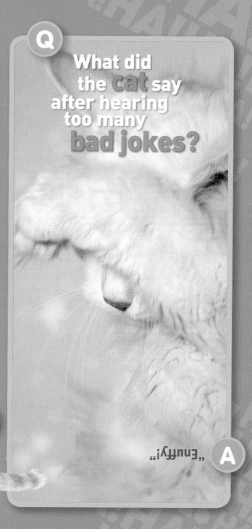

A "Enuff!"

Q Why couldn't the detective solve the cat burglar case?

A He was missing lynx.

Q What kind of **cat** has **twice** as many **legs** and likes to **swim?**

A An octo-puss.

Q If a car runs on gas and a phone runs on electricity, what does a jaguar run on?

A Its paws.

Q What do you call a **lynx** that gets everything it **asks** for?

A Purr-suasive.

KNOCK, KNOCK.

Who's there?
Rita.
Rita who?
Rita funny book lately?

Lynx have back legs that are longer than their front legs.

89

NAME Lucia

FAVORITE ACTIVITY
Grooming humans

FAVORITE TOY
Scrunchies

PET PEEVE
Hair spray

Q

If puppies make a dog pile, what can kittens make?

A meow-tain.

A

Superpowers Cats Wish They Had:

- Thumbs to open canned food
- Invisibility for sneak attacks
- Ability to fly faster and higher than any bird—yum!
- Mind control over humans—more treats!
- Mind control over dogs—less drool!
- Ability to time travel back to ancient Egypt

A cat's brain weighs as much as five quarters.

KNOCK, KNOCK.

Who's there?
Red.
Red who?
Red *If You Give a Mouse a Cookie?* It's my favorite cookbook.

Famous
Feline

94

NAME: Lil BUB

BREED: Domestic shorthair
(with a coat similar to a mackerel tabby)

SUPERSTAR STATUS:

Lil BUB is cuteness on a mission. She was born with genetic disorders and a rare bone disease resulting in her stubby legs and small, kitten-like size. Although she won't grow any larger, she's already a huge furry hero, raising awareness and money to support other animals with special needs. She hosts her own talk show online in which she interviews celebrities such as Whoopi Goldberg and even SUE the *T. rex* from the Field Museum in Chicago, Illinois, U.S.A. In her free time, Lil BUB is busy meeting fans and bringing joy in her own big way.

Lil BUB travels by car and plane while sitting in her owner's lap—or occasionally on his shoulder.

Her cute tongue hangs out because her teeth never grew in.

Lil BUB is a polydactyl cat, which means she has extra toes—one additional toe on each of her four paws.

TONGUE TWISTER!

Say this fast three times:

Ten kittens in ten mittens.

Q When is a cat driving in style?

A When it's behind the wheel of a Jaguar.

Q Why does a leopard never remember your birthday?

A It has a spotty memory.

Cat TALK

I GOT ANTLERS. YOU GOT A SLEIGH?

Naughty PETS
CAUGHT ON CAMERA

NAME Tarzan

FAVORITE ACTIVITY
Finding new uses for boring human items

FAVORITE TOY
Curtain tassels

PET PEEVE
Getting claws stuck

CURTAINS? I THOUGHT THIS WAS A CLIMBING WALL FOR MY PLAYROOM.

Cats purr at frequencies that can help heal their bodies and improve their bone density.

99

Q What does a **family** of **cats** look for when moving to a **new home?**

A A mice family next door that they can have over for dinner.

A Cat's Life Goals:

- Get more sleep—so tired from sleeping all day
- Catch red laser and destroy it for all catkind!
- Become an Internet superstar
- Jump into a cardboard box, then jump out, then repeat
- Perfect tuna fish sandwich recipe
- Create exclusive line of claw-marked furniture

Q

What does a
one-ton
(0.9-MT)
chipmunk
say when it
walks through
the neighborhood?

"Here, kitty, kitty."

A

Say this fast three times:

Catnap on a Knapsack.

Q What nursery rhyme do kittens like best?

A "Three Blind Mice."

Q How does a margay clean its coat?

A With a cat-a-comb.

Q What does a cat call a mouse?

A Delicious.

102

Onions are poisonous
to cats.

103

Cat TALK

YUCK, IS THIS THE *DIRTY* LAUNDRY PILE? YOU SAY MY LITTER BOX IS STINKY? WHAT ARE THEY FEEDING *YOU*?

Langue de chat, the name of a long thin cookie, means "cat tongue" in French.

Why do cheetahs and leopards dislike playing hide-and-seek? **Q**

A Because they're always spotted.

HILLARY: Did you hear about the cat that climbed into a UFO?
CHRIS: No. Why would it do that?
HILLARY: It spaced out.

All cats, no matter the breed, are born with blue eyes. Their true eye color appears at about 12 weeks.

KNOCK, KNOCK.

Who's there?
Sam.
Sam who?
Sam cat that knocked earlier.

Q

What does a **cat** drink during the **summer?**

A

Mice tea.

Q

Why should cats win Olympic gold medals?

A

Because they can lap water faster than any swimmer.

108

Q

What has stripes and bounces really high?

A A tabby on a trampoline.

TONGUE TWISTER!

Say this fast three times:

Black cat's back, **brown** cat's back.

Q

What do you get when you cross leopard cubs with lambs?

A Spotted wool socks.

Q

Why was the cat sad?

A Because it was a Russian blue.

110

YEAH, UM ... NEXT TIME, CAN YOU TRY NOT TO GET YOUR HAIR ALL OVER THIS SWEATER? IT REALLY MESSES UP THE LOOK I'M GOING FOR HERE.

Cat TALK

Bare-naked Sphynx cats don't have any whiskers.

KNOCK, KNOCK.

Who's there?
Ben.
Ben who?
Ben looking for a hand to pet me!

Kittens must be held and petted every day between the ages of two and eight weeks, or they will remain wild forever.

Q

Why do cats chase after the ice-cream truck?

A

For the mice-cream sandwiches.

SARA: What do you call something that's half lion and half vacuum?
CONRAD: A good reason to keep my room clean!

Famous ★★ ★Feline

NAME: Nyan Cat
BREED: Cross between a Russian blue and a pastry

SUPERSTAR STATUS:

Combine a cat with a pastry and then animate him to fly through space while a Japanese pop song plays. It sounds like a very odd way to start your morning, and that doesn't include the rainbow trail. Before it became a world-famous animation, Nyan Cat was just a whimsical illustration called Pop Tart Cat. But like any complete breakfast, Nyan Cat led to big things—like more than four million fans, some of whom have designed their own Nyan Cat computer programs and video games.

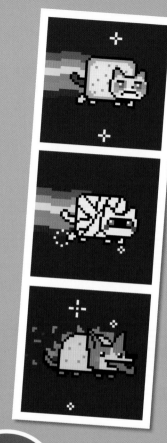

Nyan Cat comes in more than 30 different "flavors"—different designs and songs.

One flavor is Nyan Cat dressed as a mummy.

Another flavor is a taco-dog hybrid.

117

Q Why didn't the cat climb up the tree?

A It's rough bark scared it away.

Say this fast three times:

Gabby's flabby tabby grabbed a crab.

Q What has two legs, a fur coat, and looks like half a tiger?

A The other half of the tiger.

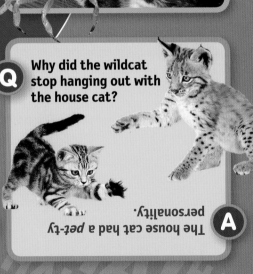

Q Why did the wildcat stop hanging out with the house cat?

A The house cat had a pet-ty personality.

KNOCK, KNOCK.

Who's there?
Daryl.
Daryl who?
Daryl be a lot more jokes coming your way!

A cat's eye has three eyelids.

119

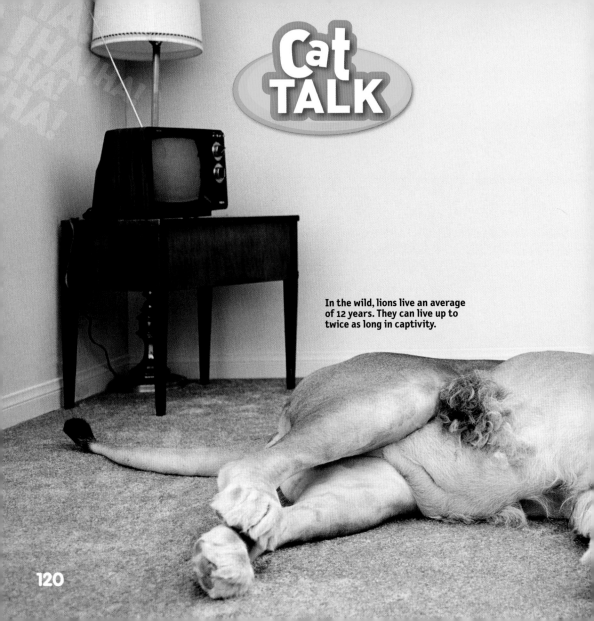

Cat
TALK

In the wild, lions live an average of 12 years. They can live up to twice as long in captivity.

121

Q What card game do fishing cats like to play?

A Go Fish!

Q What do cats like on their fish sticks?

A Catsup.

Q Which cat makes a good waitress?

A A serv-all.

Q Why did the kids give away their parents?

A The cat was allergic.

122

A wealthy Italian woman left $13 million to her cat, Tommaso.

KNOCK, KNOCK.

Who's there?
Hyde.
Hyde who?
Hyde like to tell you another joke.

123

Naughty PETS — CAUGHT ON CAMERA

NAMES Marco and Polo

FAVORITE ACTIVITY
Unwrapping presents

FAVORITE TOY
Gift bags

PET PEEVE
Double-sided tape

Kittens are always in the mood for fun. They spend almost every waking minute playing.

125

Q

Which feline did King Midas want as a pet?

A

A golden cat.

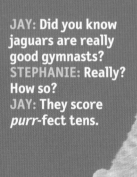

JAY: Did you know jaguars are really good gymnasts?
STEPHANIE: Really? How so?
JAY: They score *purr*-fect tens.

126

Cats have been domesticated for at least 4,000 years.

127

Cat TALK

Cheetahs can accelerate to 70 miles an hour (113 km/h)—that's as fast as a car speeding on a highway.

What Your Cat Steals When You're Not Looking:

- One left sock
- One right slipper
- Two of your fish sticks
- The dog's lunch money
- The extra roll of toilet paper
- Your math homework—blames it on the dog

BAD CAT
657679

JIMMY: Do you think Luke Skywalker favors cats or dogs?
AARON: Definitely cats.
JIMMY: Why do you say that?
AARON: Because his childhood pet was a lightsaber-toothed cat.

Q How did the **birthday boy** find out about his **present?**

A His dad let the cat out of the gift bag.

131

Q What's a cat's favorite cooking tool?

A A whisker.

Say this fast three times:

A little ditty by an itty-bitty kitty.

Q What was the headline when the cat burglar confessed that his crimes were not committed alone?

A Cat Burglar Lynx Lion Cheetah.

Q Why are cats no longer allowed to drive cars?

A Too many *hiss-and-runs*.

132

Sir Isaac Newton, the British scientist who discovered gravity in 1687, also invented the cat door.

133

Short legs and a chunky body make a Pallas's cat more suited to slinking than to running like a cheetah. A Pallas's cat relies on the ability to creep very close to prey, unnoticed, and then pounce.

What kind of feline lives with kings and queens?

A Pallas's cat.

135

Q

Why did the sand cat get so many letters in December?

A

Because it had sandy claws.

WHO'S THE KING OF THE JUNGLE NOW, HUH?

Cat TALK

Every day 70,000 puppies and kittens are born in the United States.

KNOCK, KNOCK.

Who's there?
Hugh.
Hugh who?
Hugh make me purr.

137

Famous ★★ ★Feline

NAME: Garfield

BREED: Cartoon

SUPERSTAR STATUS:

Unlike most house cats, Garfield loves a lasagna buffet, drinks coffee, and despises Mondays. The animated fat feline is always giving sharp-witted replies to his foolish owner, Jon; teasing Odie the dog; or simply resting between snack times. Since 1978, this pasta-loving *purr*-sonality has been huge in stomach size and popularity. He's gotten his paws into everything from books and parades to movies and postage stamps. Garfield even has a Guinness World Record for the most widely syndicated comic strip in the world. Not too shabby for a lazy cat who claims eating and sleeping as his highlights. The best part of his worldwide fame may be that his comic is translated into 40 languages—*purr*-fect for ordering heaps of the local cuisine wherever he goes.

Garfield was born in an Italian restaurant.

Jim Davis, the creator of Garfield, modeled Garfield's behavior on the 25 farm cats he grew up with and on some of his grandfather's personality traits.

There's only one food Garfield dislikes: raisins.

139

ALEX: I have a great dog joke for you.
TAMMI: Okay, let's hear it!
ALEX: Just kitten!

Q How do cats order new toys?

A From a catalog.

Q What happened when the **lion**, the **leopard**, and the **cheetah** got caught in a **thunderstorm?**

A They got wet, silly.

Q Why did the cats follow the leader?

A They were copycats.

NauGHty PETS **CAUGHT ON CAMERA**

PUT THE DRUMSTICKS NEXT TO ME. I'LL EAT LUNCH AFTER MY NAP.

NAME **Mr. Fudge**

FAVORITE ACTIVITY
Dreaming about his next meal

FAVORITE TOY
Hamburger-shaped pillow

PET PEEVE
When "ketchup" is spelled C-A-T-S-U-P

Cougars use their long, thick tails for balance as they run and when they climb trees and rocks.

What steps do you take if a mountain lion is chasing you?

Big ones!

143

Q How do you know when it's raining cats and dogs?

A The wind howls and you're feline wet.

WHO POSTED A PHOTO OF ME IN A DIAPER? UNTAG! UNTAG!

Cat TALK

144

KNOCK, KNOCK.

Who's there?
Hammond.
Hammond who?
Hammond cheese would be great for lunch.

Pets Deli in Berlin, Germany, serves gourmet meals for dogs and cats.

WHAT DO YOU MEAN THE BLOW-DRYER IS NOW OFF-LIMITS? HOW ELSE WILL I CREATE THIS MAGNIFICENT POOFINESS?

Cat TALK

Q Where can your cat lay down, but you can't?

A Your lap.

Say this fast three times:

Six slick Siberian lynx look left.

Q Where do cats like to go on school field trips?

A To a *meow-seum.*

Q What kind of cat becomes a doctor?

A A first-aid kit-ten.

Because ancient Egyptians believed cats protected homes and children from danger, nearly all households had a cat.

149

Q What did the cat say during the Shakespeare play?

A "Tabby or not tabby."

Say this fast three times:

Which switch did the cat's witch pick?

Q Which side of an ocelot has the most spots?

A The outside.

Q Why are **cats** so **popular?**

A Because they're **purr**-fect.

150

151

Missi, the cat with the world's longest whisker, has a whisker that is longer than a dollar bill, reaching a record 5.7 inches (14.5 cm) long.

153

Three cats are trick-or-treating. The first cat says, "I just got a 3 Mouse-keteers bar! What did you get?" The second cat replies, "I got a Kit Cat bar! What did you get?" The third cat frowns and says, "I got a dog bone."

Q

Where did the cat go when it lost its tail?

A To a retail store.

Q How does a cat cut the grass?

A It uses a lawn meow-er.

REALLY, WE'RE ALL GOING TO WEAR THE SAME SHIRT? AWK-WARD...

Cat TALK

KNOCK, KNOCK.

Who's there?
Colin.
Colin who?
Colin all
cat lovers!

Some scientists
believe that cats
can hear the
ultrasonic sounds
that come before
an earthquake.

Cats communicate using at least 16 known "cat words."

OF COURSE I CAN KEEP A SECRET!

Cat
TALK

Famous
Feline

NAME: Sam

BREED: Domestic shorthair

SUPERSTAR STATUS:

If you can tell a lot about humans from their eyes, then you can tell a lot about Sam the cat from his eyebrows. The two simple black markings on his forehead have made Sam Instagram-famous for looking curious, sad, hopeful, and worried. What calms his furry nerves? People! He enjoys playing and is happiest when someone's nearby. If you duck down and slowly approach him, Sam will tilt his head, arch his back, and jump up. After running a lap around the house, he'll come back ready for more. And Sam's fans will be ready for more posts of those eyebrows in action.

Sam is a big cat, weighing 11.4 pounds (5.17 kg)—that's more than some small dogs!

Sam doesn't like hats.

To be close to his owners while they're outside gardening, Sam relaxes in a pet stroller.

Q Why did the cat do so well on the test?

A It was *hiss-tory.*

Q How does a cat chorus warm up?

A It sings *do-re-meow.*

A litter of kittens is also called a kindle.

KNOCK, KNOCK.

Who's there?
Waddle.
Waddle who?
Waddle you do if I don't tell you the punch line?

163

How did the queen drive her kittens to school?

In a Cat-illac.

A cat's top speed is about 31 miles an hour (50 km/h).

Q

What happened when the margay drank lemonade?

A

It became a sourpuss.

JAMIE: Guess what? My cat got first place at the bird show!

STEVEN: How did she do that?

JAMIE: She jumped up onstage and snatched the winning bird right out of its owner's hand.

A 15-year-old cat has probably spent 10 years of its life sleeping.

KNOCK, KNOCK.

Who's there?
Dishes.
Dishes who?
Dishes the most knock-knock jokes I've ever told.

A cat can jump about five to seven times its own height.

Things Cats Would Invent:

- A bird feeder that feeds birds to cats
- A remote-controlled squirrel-chasing robot
- Tabby-lets—mobile devices designed especially for cat paws
- Tail-toppers—little hats for tall, dashing tails
- A third hand on humans so they can pet, feed, and play at the same time

PRIYANKA: What's the difference between a lion and your dad?
EDDIE: I don't know. What?
PRIYANKA: One roars and the other snores.

Q Which cat performs on a trapeze?

A An acro-cat.

TONGUE TWISTER!

Say this fast three times:

Phil flees from friendly felines.

Q Why wouldn't you want to **play** against a **team** of **big cats?**

A They might be cheetahs.

Q When Cinderella went to the ball, who fed her cat?

A Her furry godmother.

KNOCK, KNOCK.

Who's there?
Ivan.
Ivan who?
Ivan idea for something new to scratch today.

Some of the best cat toys are free: a crumpled-up newspaper on the floor or a paper bag.

173

NAUGHty PETS

CAUGHT ON CAMERA

NAME Hemingway

FAVORITE ACTIVITY
Dreaming about being in charge of all the lions in the world

FAVORITE TOY
Sleeping bag filled with catnip

PET PEEVE
Alarm clocks

REMEMBER THAT TIME, LIKE FIVE MINUTES AGO, WHEN YOU WOKE UP AND I WAS SLEEPING ON YOUR FACE? HA-HA! I'M HILARIOUS!

Cat TALK

Q In what month do cats eat the least?

A February—it's the shortest month.

TONGUE TWISTER!

Say this fast three times:

Fishing cats try fresh flat flounder.

Q When is it bad luck to pass a black cat's path?

A When you're a mouse.

Mother cats nurse their kittens until they're ready to eat other food.

KNOCK,

KNOCK.

Who's there?
Carrie.
Carrie who?
Carrie a kitten
in your mouth
before?

Cats have no collarbone, which gives them a flexible skeleton. This means they can twist and turn even in midair, like when they flip their bodies during a fall, trying to land on their feet.

Can a **cat** ballroom dance?

Q

A *Paws-ibly!*

Q Where do the noisiest cats come from?

A Purr-sia.

Q Where did the artist display his cat statue?

A On a cat-er-pillar.

180

About 10 percent of a cat's bones are in its tail.

KNOCK, KNOCK.

Who's there?
Olive.
Olive who?
Olive curling up on your lap.

181

Famous ★★ ★ Feline

182

NAME: Snoopy

BREED: Exotic shorthair

SUPERSTAR STATUS:

This may be the Internet's most fashionable feline. Snoopy the cat is a model in many ways, from his unique look to his range of accessories. He's been photographed showing off hats, sweaters, socks, and even fancy necklaces. Everything matches Snoopy's flat face and innocent-looking eyes. Maybe one day this ultracool kitty will be on a catwalk in *Mew*-lan, Italy.

His owner calls Snoopy's best feature his "pie face."

Snoopy lives in China.

His parents were an American shorthair and a Persian cat.

183

Why couldn't the cat pay its vet bill?

Q

A He was paw.

A tortoiseshell sees a seashell.

Q Why was the cat excited about the new computer?

A It was told it came with a mouse.

Q What did the **snake** say when the **sand cat** bit its **tail?**

A "That's the end of me!"

When doing difficult tasks, female cats tend to be right-pawed, whereas males are usually left-pawed.

KNOCK, KNOCK.

Who's there?
Sabina.
Sabina who?
Sabina long time since I pawed your furry face.

185

Americans spend one and a half times more money on pet food than on baby food.

Q Which vegetables do cats prefer?

A As-purr-agus

187

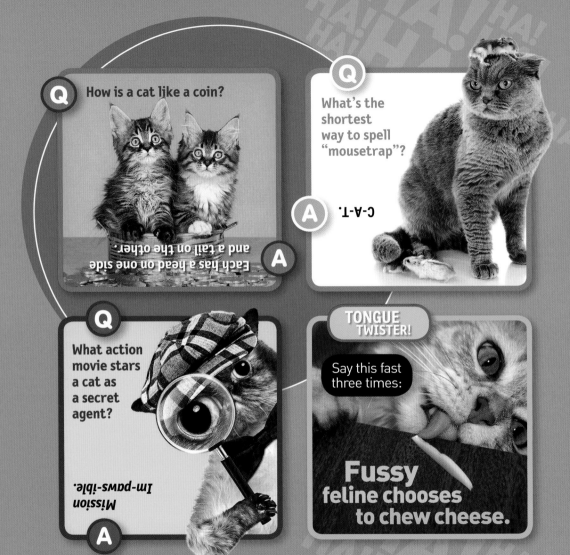

Q How is a cat like a coin?

A Each has a head on one side and a tail on the other.

Q What's the shortest way to spell "mousetrap"?

A C-A-T.

Q What action movie stars a cat as a secret agent?

A Mission Im-paws-ible.

TONGUE TWISTER!

Say this fast three times:

Fussy feline chooses to chew cheese.

KNOCK, KNOCK.

Who's there?
Howard.
Howard who?
Howard I ever resist your garden's catnip?

At some pet spas, cats are treated to catnip tea.

Cats are nearsighted. What humans can see clearly at a distance will look blurry to a cat.

NOPE, I DEFINITELY HAVEN'T SEEN YOUR GLASSES.

Cat TALK

Q Why did the lion buy a new suit?

A It took pride in its appearance.

Q Which "Peanuts" character do cats like best?

A Lioness.

Q Why did the two cats dress alike?

A They were Siamese twins.

TONGUE TWISTER!

Say this fast three times:

A bobcat can't can-can.

Cats see six times better at night than humans do.

KNOCK, KNOCK.

Who's there?
Kenya.
Kenya who?
Kenya see me under the covers?

193

Famous ★★
★ Feline

NAME: Nala

BREED: Siamese/domestic shorthair mix

SUPERSTAR STATUS:

For the most part, Nala is an average cat. She likes to nap on her back, enjoys belly rubs, and was adopted from a shelter. But your average cat doesn't have nearly two million followers on Instagram. Maybe they're as excited about Nala as she is about sharks. After all, she has a shark hat, a shark costume, and even a cardboard house shaped like a shark. Given that she lives in Los Angeles, California, U.S.A., maybe Nala is preparing for her Hollywood summer thriller: *Claws.*

She plays fetch like a dog.

Nala once met Lil BUB.

Nala usually waits at the front door for her owner to come home.

KNOCK, KNOCK.

Who's there?
Eiffel.
Eiffel who?
Eiffel soft
and furry.

Persians are the most popular cat breed. They make up three-quarters of all registered purebred cats.

Funny Cat Names:

- King Claw
- Mr. Furrypants
- Munch Munch
- Minnie Meowse
- Princess Purrscilla
- Pawla Purrkins

HELLO
my name is
RON FLEASLY

MEGAN: Do your cats get along?
COURTNEY: Yes, but sometimes they fight.
MEGAN: What happens then?
COURTNEY: Oh, they always hiss and make up.

Tigers and house cats share 95 percent of the same genes.

KNOCK, KNOCK.

Who's there?
Justin.
Justin who?
Justin case you want to pet me, I'm always ready.

199

Both cats and dogs tend to circle an area two or three times before lying down.

JOKEFINDER

Story jokes

Tongue twisters

ILLUSTRATION CREDITS

Published by National Geographic Partners, LLC. All rights reserved.
Reproduction of the whole or any part of the contents without written
permission from the publisher is prohibited.

Staff for This Book

Kate Olesin, *Project Editor*
Julide Dengel, *Art Director*
Rosie Gowsell Pattison, *Designer*
Hillary Leo, *Photo Editor*
Kelley Miller, *Writer*
Paige Towler, *Editorial Assistant*
Sanjida Rashid and Rachel Kenny, *Design Production Assistants*
Michaela Weglinski, *Special Projects Assistant*
Tammi Colleary-Loach, *Rights Clearance Manager*
Michael Cassady and Mari Robinson, *Rights Clearance Specialists*
Grace Hill, *Managing Editor*
Alix Inchausti, *Production Editor*
Lewis R. Bassford, *Production Manager*
Rachel Faulise, *Manager, Production Services*
Susan Borke, *Legal and Business Affairs*

Senior Management Team, Kids Publishing and Media

Nancy Laties Feresten, *Senior Vice President*
Erica Green, *Vice President, Editorial Director*
Jennifer Emmett, *Vice President, Content*
Eva Absher-Schantz, *Vice President, Visual Identity*
Amanda Larsen, *Design Director, Kids Books*
Rachel Buchholz, *Editor and Vice President,* NG Kids *magazine*
Jay Sumner, *Photo Director*
Hannah August, *Marketing Director*
R. Gary Colbert, *Production Director*

Digital

Laura Goertzel, *Manager*
Sara Zeglin, *Senior Producer*
Bianca Bowman, *Assistant Producer*
Natalie Jones, *Senior Product Manager*

Since 1888, the National Geographic Society has funded more than 12,000
research, exploration, and preservation projects around the world. The
Society receives funds from National Geographic Partners, LLC, funded in
part by your purchase. A portion of the proceeds from this book supports
this vital work. To learn more, visit natgeo.com/info.

NATIONAL GEOGRAPHIC and Yellow Border Design are trademarks of the
National Geographic Society, used under license.

For more information, please visit nationalgeographic.com,
call 1-800-647-5463, or write to the following address:
National Geographic Partners
1145 17th Street N.W.
Washington, D.C. 20036-4688 U.S.A.

Visit us online at nationalgeographic.com/books

For librarians and teachers: ngchildrensbooks.org

More for kids from National Geographic: natgeokids.com

For information about special discounts for bulk purchases, please contact
National Geographic Books Special Sales: specialsales@natgeo.com

For rights or permissions inquiries, please contact National Geographic
Books Subsidiary Rights: bookrights@natgeo.com

Trade paperback ISBN: 978-1-4263-2327-0
Reinforced library edition ISBN: 978-1-4263-2328-7

Printed in China
18/PPS/2